Lighthou

England

The North East

The lighthouses of Northumberland, Durham, Yorkshire and Humberside

Tony Denton and Nicholas Leach

▲ The well known St Mary's lighthouse, north of the entrance to the river Tyne.

◄ (Front cover) Longstone lighthouse in the Outer Farne Islands.

◄ (Frontispiece) Souter lighthouse.

Published by
Foxglove Media
Foxglove House
Shute Hill
Lichfield
Staffordshire WS13 8DB
England
Tel (01543) 673594

© Nicholas Leach and Tony Denton 2010

British Library Cataloguing in Publication Data. A catalogue record for this book is available from the British Library.

ISBN 978-0-9513656-6-3

Layout and design by Nicholas Leach
Printed by Cromwell Press Group, Trowbridge

Contents

Lighthouse History

This book provides a comprehensive guide to the lighthouses and harbour lights along the north-east coast of England, starting with the most northerly light in England at Berwick-upon-Tweed, and going south to the Humber Estuary. This group of lighthouses includes some notable architectural towers, many of which are both famous in their own right, such as Longstone, and historically significant, such as Spurn Point. The different structures built to display lights and safeguard mariners range from the sturdy stone structures of offshore towers to the harbour beacons on lattice poles displayed in small ports.

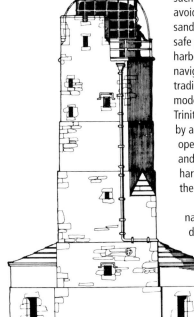

▶ The seventeenth century tower at Tynemouth, built with stone from the ruins of the nearby priory, as it appeared around the 1840s. It was demolished in 1898 having been replaced by the lighthouse at St Mary's to the north.

While the Corporation of Trinity House is responsible for many of these lights, including all the major ones, many significant harbour lights, both small and large, are also in operation, and full details of these have been included. This introduction provides a general overview of lighthouse development and organisation in England and Wales, focussing on the need for lights to mark England's east coast, as well as explaining how Trinity House has developed into the service it is today.

The first lights

Trading by sea has been a principal activity of all civilisations, yet moving goods and cargoes by water involves facing difficulties and dangers such as storms and bad weather, avoiding reefs, headlands, sandbanks and cliffs, and making safe passage into ports and harbours. The need for aids to navigation is therefore as old as trading by sea itself and, today, modern lighthouses operated by Trinity House are supplemented by a plethora of small, locally-operated lights of varying sizes and range, mainly around ports, harbours and estuaries, to aid the safety of vessels.

The earliest aids to navigation were beacons or daymarks, sited near harbours or ports rather than on headlands or reefs, to help ships reach their destination safely. The earliest lighthouses were

in the Mediterranean, and the oldest such structure of which written records survive was that on the island of Pharos, off Alexandria, on the northern coast of Egypt. The Pharos lighthouse, which stands 466ft tall, was built between 283BC and 247BC and stood until 1326.

The development of lighthouses around the coasts of the British Isles mirrored the expansion of trade routes. The earliest British lights were built on the south and east coasts to assist vessels trading with European and French ports. But by the seventeenth century, the emphasis had changed, with lights along the east coast established to help guide colliers carrying coal from the ports of the north-east to London, the burgeoning capital.

The coal trade from Newcastle and Sunderland to London dominated coastal traffic. Between 1760 and 1830 the tonnage of ships engaged in the trade increased more than

▲ The lighthouse at North Shields, above Fish Quay, at the entrance to the river Tyne was built in 1727 and is now a private dwelling.

▶ Although it had been completed, the North Pier at Tynemouth was breached in 1897. As a result it was not formally opened until 1910. The lighthouse at the end was effectively on an island during this time.

fourfold, and as much as forty per cent of coastal shipping in the period 1779 to 1884 was devoted to coal carriage. Indeed, the coal trade was the largest single activity of coastal shipping during the industrial revolution. The busiest shipping lane was down the east coast, which, according to shipping historian Ralph Davis, 'though plagued by storms and hazardous shoals, [it] often formed the most direct line of communication between important commercial centres'.

The greater number of ships putting to sea increased the incidence of shipwrecks, particularly as colliers were often poorly maintained and risked the hazards of the seas more often than was advisable. Shipping might be held up in the major ports for weeks during storms, and those that did venture out could be wrecked if caught out by unexpected severe weather. On several occasions during this period, accounts record hundreds of merchant sailing ships being wrecked in single storms.

Attempts to reduce the hazards led to the first efforts at improving safety in and around Britain's ports. At the busiest ports and the most travelled shipping lanes improvements were urgently needed.

▼ An early drawing of Flamborough lighthouse and part of the headland on which it was built.

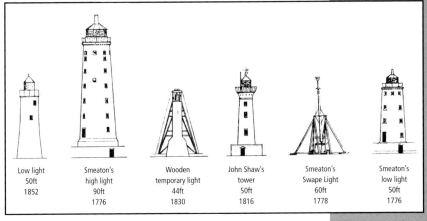

Low light 50ft 1852	Smeaton's high light 90ft 1776	Wooden temporary light 44ft 1830	John Shaw's tower 50ft 1816	Smeaton's Swape Light 60ft 1778	Smeaton's low light 50ft 1776

Lighthouses were constructed to mark the major headlands and sandbanks while, usually on a smaller scale than the great offshore and headland towers, lights were also erected at the entrances to ports, harbours and rivers. Congestion at ports had increased during the eighteenth and nineteenth centuries, and improvements to enable larger volumes of trade to be handled included measures to reduce risks to shipping, the most visible of which were lighthouses at the harbour entrances.

The first light to be erected along the north-east coast of England was probably at Spurn Point at the mouth of the Humber estuary in the early fifteenth century, although precise details of its construction and operation are lacking. A petition from William Reedbarrow, 'Heremyte of the Chapell of our Lady and Seint Anne atte Ravensersporne', addressed to Parliament in 1427, stated that a light should be shown to 'alle the Vesselx

▲ Drawings of the lighthouses of Spurn Point showing Smeaton's high lighthouse and the low lighthouses successively erected to work with it.

◄ A print from 1820 shows the Smeaton-designed high light and Shaw's tower of 1816 at Spurn Point, overlooking the river Humber.

lacking. However, it was the earliest light on the east coast, and one of the earliest aids to navigation in the British Isles.

An early set of lights on the east coast was that at the mouth of the Tyne at North Shields. Arguably the first lit leading marks in the British Isles, two towers were built in 1540 by the Trinity House of Newcastle, under a charter of 1536 from Henry VIII who authorised the levy of dues for their maintenance. It provided that the members of the local Trinity House Corporation, which had existed since 1492, might 'found, build, make and frame of stone, lime and sand, by the best ways and means that they knew or can, two towers' for the safety of the users of the port. Though intended partly for defence, the towers indicated a navigable channel of the Tyne to mariners when they kept them in line.

Trinity House

The organisation responsible for the operation and maintenance of the major aids to navigation today is the Corporation of Trinity House. The exact origins of Trinity House are obscure, but probably date back to the early thirteenth century, when groups of tradesmen, such as seamen, masters of merchant vessels and pilots, formed guilds to protect their interests.

One of the first such organisations was the Deptford Trinity House, which was incorporated by royal charter after its members had petitioned Henry VIII to prohibit unqualified

that comyn into the seid Ryver of Humbre'. However, it is not known whether Reedbarrow's proposal came to anything, or even whether a light was kindled, as further details of it are entirely

pilots on the Thames in 1513. Deptford was then a busy port and the main point of entry for the capital's trade, so pilotage duties were lucrative, and Trinity House members wanted to retain their monopoly.

However, Trinity House was generally reluctant to build lighthouses. Instead it encouraged entrepreneurs to consider building them as profit-making undertakings. As a result, private lighthouse ownership

became relatively widespread during the seventeenth century and the number of private lighthouses increased during the following centuries. Choosing the best position for a light, with sufficiently busy ports nearby from which revenue could be collected, was crucial for the light to yield a good return.

Although a proliferation of unnecessary lights was prevented, private light owners gained a reputation for greed,

▲ The steel tower erected at Bamburgh in 1910 was used until 1975, when it was removed and the light transferred onto the adjacent store building.

◀ The lighthouse in Scarborough at the end of Vincent's Pier, where local paddle steamers berthed during the nineteenth century, dominates the town's harbour.

was passed giving Trinity House of Deptford Strond complete authority over aids to navigation. The body was also responsible for sanctioning the position and character of any lights managed by other organisations, which had to apply to Trinity House for permission before erecting a light. Although the majority of English lights were already under the jurisdiction of Trinity House, the 1836 Act centralised lighthouse management.

The Act also gave Trinity House the power to purchase all privately-owned lights. Although by that time only ten lighthouses remained in private ownership, the compensation paid to owners cost the Corporation a staggering £1,182,546. On the east coast the lights at Tynemouth and Spurn Point were privately owned, and they had given their respective proprietors a handsome income for many years.

In 1832 the Spurn lights were bringing surplus dues of £8,958 per annum to owners Benedict John Angell and George Lowther Thomson, who managed the lights under an act of parliament in perpetuity. In the same year the Tynemouth light achieved a net surplus of £2,693 for its proprietor, William Fowke. After negotiations, Trinity House paid £309,531 to take over the Spurn light, and £124,678 for that at Tynemouth, both considerable sums at the time.

Once the private lighthouses had been wholly taken over, Trinity House assumed control of lighthouse maintenance

▲ The lighthouse at Withernsea is very unusual in that it is situated amongst terraced housing a quarter of a mile from the coast, with the majority of the town's buildings closer to the sea. It was one of a number of impressive lighthouses built by Trinity House towards the end of the nineteenth century.

and lights were built on a haphazard basis. As a result, large areas of the coastline remained unlit, and by the nineteenth century, with the level of trade increasing as Britain's industry expanded, the situation was clearly unacceptable. Trinity House had to accept the new demands and, with the leases expiring on many privately-owned lighthouses, the Corporation was forced to take over many sites. In 1824 the lease on the three Farne lights, off the coast of Northumberland, was purchased for £36,446 with fifteen years still to run.

The changes in lighthouse administration were formalised in 1836, when an Act of Parliament

and construction throughout the country. During the great period of lighthouse construction between 1870 and 1900, Victorian engineers and designers constructed and modernised at least fifty stations and built new rock towers.

A number of impressive new lighthouses were built on the east coast during this era, most notably those at St Mary's, Souter and Withernsea. The light at Souter was shown from a particularly fine tower and the whole station was a model of lighthouse engineering. It witnessed some innovative design solutions, and was fitted with a series of lenses which multiplied the original light 230 times. The support buildings housed a small army of people and included no fewer than six houses for the keepers together with their families.

Harbour lights

Much of the literature about lighthouses has concentrated on the major lights,

such as Souter, as these are often impressive structures and many are in spectacular locations. However, no less important are the many smaller lights found at most ports and harbours. They have been built in response to specific local circumstances, so their design and purpose differ markedly and the variety of lights is considerable.

Many harbour authorities are responsible for their own aids to navigation, and this has led to a variety of lights and beacons being erected. Some ports, where

▲ The lighthouse at St Mary's Island when in service. The tower is 120ft tall, and its light had a range of seventeen miles.

▼ The compressed air-driven diaphone foghorn at Flamborough was superseded by an electric apparatus in 1975.

vessels need to follow channels, have leading or range lights which, when aligned, mark a safe passage. Others have long piers or breakwaters, the limits of which need marking, and on these some of the finest light towers have been constructed, such as that at Tynemouth.

Along the north-east coast of England, where trade between ports was competitive, when new harbours and breakwaters were constructed grand lighthouses were also part of the works to mark their entrances, such as the significant towers erected at Sunderland and

Whitby. At other ports along the coast more functional lights have been erected, such as those at Berwick, Hartlepool and the Tees.

Lightkeepers

Throughout the history of lighthouses, the lightkeeper has played an essential role in maintaining the light. However, during the latter half of the twentieth century the era of manned lighthouses came to an end as automation became the norm for aids to navigation.

But, before automation, every light had to be operated by at least two keepers. The idealised view of lighthouse keepers conjures up a somewhat romantic image of men living in a tower with only the sea for company. While this was accurate for rock stations, where keepers were confined to fairly cramped quarters, the reality for most was a little different. The lights on the mainland had a senior keeper supported by two assistant keepers, and families.

East Coast Lighthouses

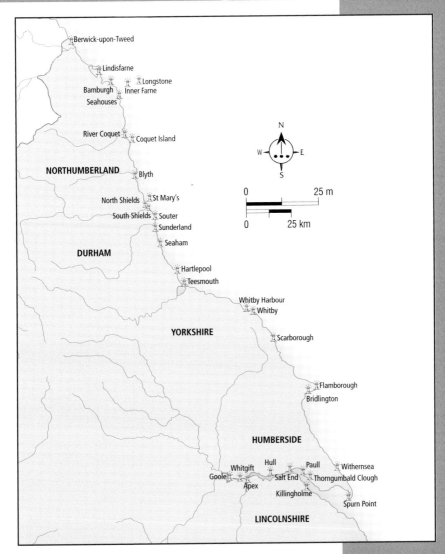

Berwick-upon-Tweed
Lindisfarne
Bamburgh
Seahouses
Longstone
Inner Farne
River Coquet
Coquet Island

NORTHUMBERLAND
Blyth
North Shields
St Mary's
South Shields
Souter
Sunderland
Seaham

DURHAM
Hartlepool
Teesmouth

Whitby Harbour
Whitby

YORKSHIRE
Scarborough

Flamborough
Bridlington

HUMBERSIDE
Whitgift
Hull
Paull
Withernsea
Goole
Salt End
Thorngumbald Clough
Apex
Killingholme
Spurn Point

LINCOLNSHIRE

N
W — E
S

0 ____ 25 m

0 ____ 25 km

The guide to the lighthouses starts at Berwick-upon-Tweed on the border with Scotland, and runs south through Northumberland and Yorkshire, ending with the lights of the Humber. The photographs show the lighthouses as they are today, and a number of historic images have also been included. The information about visiting the lights should be used only as a starting point. Consulting road atlases and Ordnance Survey maps is advisable when visiting any of the places. The map above is for information only to indicate the lighthouses' overall location.

Berwick-upon-Tweed

ESTABLISHED
1826

CURRENT TOWER
1826

OPERATOR
Berwick-upon-
Tweed Harbour
Commissioners

ACCESS
By walking the
breakwater with care
as the ramparts are
unguarded

▶▶ Berwick's
lighthouse at
the end of the
breakwater dates
from 1826.

▼ The lighthouse at
Berwick is the most
northerly in England.

Between 1147 and 1482 the township of Berwick-upon-Tweed passed to and fro between Scotland and England thirteen times before eventually being acquired by England following its capture by Richard Duke of Gloucester, the future King Richard III. Although not officially merged into England, the town has been administered by England ever since.

During the late eighteenth and early nineteenth centuries the town became a prosperous port and market centre, and the harbour was gradually improved. The quays were extended and protection against the north wind was provided by a long breakwater, which was constructed in 1810-11.

In 1826 what is now the most northerly lighthouse in England was built on the end of the new breakwater.

Built to the design of Joseph Nelson, it is a 43ft stone-built tapered circular tower with a conical top made out of one piece of solid stone. Painted mainly white, it has a red band at the base and a red roof. The light, which is operated by Berwick-upon-Tweed Harbour Commissioners, shows a flashing white light every five seconds visible for ten miles through a seaward-facing window with a small gallery. There is a fixed green light visible for one mile which shines through a landward-facing window lower down the tower.

Lindisfarne

ESTABLISHED
circa 1820

OPERATOR
Trinity House

ACCESS
The Guile Point beacons can be reached via a three-mile walk heading north from the hamlet of Ross but can also be seen from the Heugh Hill light on Holy Island which overlooks Lindisfarne Priory

►► The West Law obelisk, used as a daymark, is situated over 100 yards from the east obelisk.

▼ The two stone obelisks at Guile Point, seen from Holy Island, mark the south-eastern entrance to the island's harbour.

When limestone and coal were beginning to be carried by sea during the first half of the nineteenth century, the harbour on the south side of Holy Island grew increasingly busy. However, many ships ran aground off the island, often mistaking Emmanuel Head, on the island's north-eastern corner, for the Lindisfarne channel. To counter this, a 48ft white-painted stone pyramid was erected on the headland to act as a daymark. Believed to be the first such structure on the coast, it assisted with the approach to the harbour from the north.

Around the same time, two daymarks or beacons in the form of obelisks were erected at Guile Point on the mainland side of the harbour entrance, to the south of Holy Island. These beacons, topped with triangular daymarks, aided vessels involved in the coal and lime trades by marking the southern approach to Lindisfarne harbour. Designed for Trinity House by John Dobson, the beacons were built between 1820 and 1840 and, known as East and West Law, were respectively 70ft and 83ft in height and 122 yards apart. When aligned, they marked a safe southern approach into the harbour. Vessels would follow this course until reaching a point where the Heugh Beacon aligned with the belfry of St Mary's Church. At this point, course would be altered to follow the narrow channel, which led to the anchorage.

Shifting sands subsequently made the beacons inaccurate, and the East Law was discontinued in 1995, when a fixed light with a range of four miles was attached a third of the way up the West Law tower. This light, under the control of Trinity House, is known as Guile Point light. It is supplemented by a new light, with a range of five miles, built to carry out the duties of the original East Law pyramid and sited on the opposite side of the channel on Holy Island close to Lindisfarne Priory. Known as Heugh Hill, it helps to mark the channel into Lindisfarne Harbour.

Bamburgh

ESTABLISHED
1910

CURRENT TOWER
1975

AUTOMATED
1975

OPERATOR
Trinity House

ACCESS
Situated at the end
of The Wynding, a
narrow road out of
Bamburgh village

▶▶ Bamburgh's
small lighthouse is
north of the village.

▼ This squat
building at
Bamburgh houses
Trinity House's most
northerly lighthouse.

The small lighthouse at Bamburgh is situated on the shore edge at Black Rock Point to the north of the town's famous castle. The Bamburgh area, and in particular the famous and imposing castle, has played an important role in English history since the occupation of the site by the Romans.

During the late eighteenth century Bamburgh Castle fell into disrepair and its buildings were used for a charity school run by a Dr Sharp. He not only set up a lifeboat station in the village, but also operated a warning system of bells and guns from the castle ramparts and, during stormy weather, employed two riders to patrol the shore and keep watch for ships in distress.

In 1910 a permanent light was established at Black Rock Point adjacent to a carbide store mounted on a 42ft black circular skeleton steel tower. The light was electrified in 1964 and in 1975 the tower was removed and the light transferred onto the store. The light is mounted 30ft above ground level in a black cylinder on the roof of the white-painted building.

The third order dioptric optic with a first order catadioptric fixed lens shows an occulting white, red and green light twice every fifteen seconds. The range of the white sector is seventeen miles, with the coloured sectors having a range of thirteen miles.

This, the most northerly land-based lighthouse in England, has never had accommodation for a keeper, and a local attendant is employed to carry out any routine maintenance.

Longstone

▶▶ Longstone
lighthouse off
the picturesque
Northumberland
coast is one of the
most famous in the
British Isles.

▼ An old postcard
showing the station
before the major
alterations 1951-2.

The Farne Islands, a small archipelago off the coast of Northumberland, consist of two distinct groups of islands separated by Staples Sound. The earliest attempt to mark the islands, a major hazard in the deepwater coastal shipping lanes, was made during the seventeenth century by Sir John Clayton, who was granted a patent to erect a light in 1669.

Four years later Clayton had a tower erected on Inner Farne as part of his scheme for lighting the east coast but, as the Newcastle merchants refused to pay any dues for its upkeep, and Trinity House did not give it their approval, its fire was never kindled. Further applications were made during the eighteenth century for a lease to build a light on the island but not until 1776 did Trinity House agree to allow Captain J. Blackett, whose family held the lease to the islands, to build two lighthouses.

The lights were exhibited for the first time on 1 September 1778. One tower, known as Cuthbert's tower, was on Inner Farne while the other was at the southern end of Staples Island and consisted of a small square cottage lighthouse. The latter building was ill sited, so was replaced in 1791 by a roughly-built coal-burning tower on nearby Brownsman's Island.

In 1796 the Staples keeper, Robert Darling, moved with his family to the new lighthouse. This light was deemed inadequate by local shipowners, while Trinity House's instruction to improve the power of the lights by fitting Argand lamps and reflectors was ignored.

The situation was clearly unsatisfactory, and by 1810 the two towers, both holding coal lights, were in a run-down state. After various discussions, the Corporation took them over and decided to have two new

Longstone

lighthouses built, one on Inner Farne and the other on Outer Farne, otherwise known as Longstone Rock, to the western side of the island group. Daniel Alexander, the Trinity House architect who succeeded Samuel Wyatt, was paid £8,500 to organise the construction work. The new light on Longstone bore one of the first revolving flashing optics in the world.

In 1822 Trinity House bought the site and four years later made major changes to the tower. The result was an enlarged red and white circular tower, 86ft in height, built of rough stone with iron railings around the lantern gallery, completed at a cost, with dwellings, of £4,771. The optic, which cost £1,441, consisted of twelve Argand lamps in parabolic reflectors and a catadioptric apparatus, and was shown for the first time in February 1826.

Longstone lighthouse is most famous as the scene of the wreck of the steamship Forfarshire, which was driven onto the Big Harcar Rocks on 7 September 1838. Grace Darling, daughter of principal keeper William Darling, saw the wreck about a mile from the lighthouse and insisted on helping her father effect a rescue.

Of sixty people on board, forty-three were drowned, but the Darlings saved nine survivors. This gallant deed turned Grace and her father into Victorian celebrities, and they were awarded a Gold medal by the Royal Humane Society.

Major alterations of 1952 saw electric generators installed, and the optics and fog signal apparatus renewed, and the station became home to a radio beacon. The white light, flashing once every twenty seconds, has a range of twenty-nine miles.

▶▶ Longstone lighthouse, which has been automatic since 1990, remains one of the most iconic of any around the coasts of the UK. Longstone be reached via boat trips from Seahouses harbour.

▼ The station during electrification works of 1951-52. Note the temporary fog signal emitters on the gallery.

Inner Farne

▶▶ The Inner Farne lighthouse is owned by the National Trust but remains fully operational with Trinity House managing the light. The white light has a range of ten miles.

▼ The lighthouse can easily be seen from the mainland on a clear day.

Inner Farne island is, at sixteen acres, the largest of the islands that make up the Farnes, off the Northumberland coast. The lighthouse was built as part of the improvements to navigation around the Farne Islands during the early years of the nineteenth century and was one of a number of lights built in the area at the time. It was completed in 1811 to the design of Daniel Alexander and consisted of a 43ft white-painted circular tower with keepers' cottages to the rear of the tower. The lantern was installed with reflectors and Argand lamps and the gallery has closely-strutted railings.

At the same time as this tower was built, a smaller tower was constructed at the north-west point of the island, about 150 yards away, and supplied with fixed white light. In 1825 Trinity House bought out the lease for the Farne lighthouse at a cost of £36,484. The light in the smaller tower was discontinued in 1910 and the present lighthouse was converted to automatic operation, with an acetylene light controlled by a sun valve. This remained in operation until the lighthouse was converted to solar power in 1996, at which point the station was also automated.

In June 2005 the National Trust bought some of the Inner Farne lighthouse buildings for £132,000 as part of an ongoing project by the Trust to acquire environmentally-sensitive areas of the north-east coastline. The acquisition included the keepers' cottages and a building used to house the generating plant when the light was powered by acetylene gas. One of the three rooms in the lighthouse complex was converted into office space for the wardens. The lighthouse itself remains operational as an aid to navigation, and the first order catadioptric fixed lens gives two white and red flashes every fifteen seconds.

Seahouses

The lighthouse built on the knuckle at the head of the north west pier in 1900 is somewhat unique in that it consists of a 25ft white-painted dome-topped octagonal brick tower with, from the land, no apparent light. The flashing green light, which is visible for twelve miles, is in fact shown from a window in the side facing the sea. There is also a fixed red light on a 20ft tripod on the breakwater head.

Seahouses is the nearest harbour to the Farne Islands, and from here both Longstone and Inner Farne lighthouses, now automated, are maintained by a local attendant.

▶▶ The small lighthouse can be seen at the end of the north-west pier.

▶ Stores building at Seahouses used by the attendants of the Farne lights.

▼ The lighthouse at the entrance to the harbour.

River Coquet

ESTABLISHED
1848

CURRENT TOWER
1848

OPERATOR
Warkworth Harbour Trust

ACCESS
The south breakwater is open to the public

►► Amble lighthouse on the south pier at the entrance to the river Coquet

▼ The two lights marking the entrance to the river Coquet and Amble harbour.

The river Coquet flows via the townships of Warkworth about a mile upstream and Amble near its mouth. Although the harbour at the entrance, built in 1838-39 by the completion of two stone breakwaters, was called Warkworth Harbour, the predominance of the larger township of Amble has led to the first section being renamed Amble. This is a little confusing as the harbour authority remains Warkworth Harbour Trust.

In the nineteenth century Warkworth was an important coal export port, and to guide ships into the river a lighthouse was erected on Coquet Island in 1841. The approach was marked in 1848 by a pair of lights on the end of the breakwaters. There is confusion as to whether the lights are called Warkworth or Amble, but for the sake of clarity the one on the south side will be referred to as Amble Breakwater Light and that on the north as Warkworth Breakwater Light.

The Amble light consists of a 31ft red and white banded cast-iron tower on a concrete base, approached by a concrete catwalk. The flashing red light shines from a solar-powered polycarbonate lamp holder mounted on top, has a range of five miles and gives a flash every six seconds. The area around the breakwater was redeveloped by Warkworth Harbour Trust in 2000 and is now a recreational site.

The Warkworth light on the north breakwater is a 27ft red lattice tower with the top section enclosed. The solar-powered flashing green light is mounted in a polycarbonate lamp holder, has a range of five miles and flashes every six seconds. The breakwater is in a poor condition and the sections each side of the light are ready to break away, and so there is no public access.

Coquet Island

►► The island
is a mile off the
Northumberland
coast. Public access
is not permitted
to either it or
the lighthouse. A
heli-pad has been
installed in the
walled area. The
island, managed by
the Royal Society
for the Protection
of Birds, is a
bird sanctuary.

► Coquet
lighthouse is on
an island on which
ecclesiastical
buildings were
built, including
a Benedictine
Monastery built in
the fifteenth century.
The fog signal gives
a three-second blast
every thirty seconds.

Coquet, a small island off the coast of Amble, was occupied by a small religious community as early as 684. Following the act of 1836, Trinity House reviewed the aids to navigation in the area and in 1841 built a lighthouse on the Island. This not only guided vessels up the east coast, but also marked the entry into the ports of Amble and Warkworth, although by 1848 these ports were marked by lights at the entrance to the river.

The very substantial tower is situated on the south-western shore of the island and cost £3,268 to construct. The sandstone castellated tower, 72ft in height and built to the design of James Walker, is surrounded by a turreted parapet with walls more than 3ft thick. The light is housed in a circular lantern room complete with conical roof and a domed ventilator.

The castellated two-storey dwelling houses were used by the keepers attending the light when the station was manned, but are now used by RSPB wardens in the bird breeding season. The whole structure was erected on the ruins of the Benedictine Monastery, parts of which were incorporated into the houses. The first keeper appointed to Coquet was William Darling, elder brother of Grace Darling, and the second of her brothers to become a keeper with Trinity House.

The light was initially fuelled by paraffin vapour with a first order fixed lens, but, when electrified in 1976, it was changed to a catadioptric gearless pedestal rotating optic, powered by eighteen sealed beam lamp units. Since automation in 1990, it has had an AGA PRB 21 optic with twelve 200W sealed beam units, and shows a white light giving three flashes every thirty seconds. The white beam is visible for twenty-one miles, with a red sector visible for sixteen miles. The fog signal, which gives a three second blast every thirty seconds, is audible for two miles.

Blyth

►► The 1788
white-painted
lighthouse at Blyth
can be found in
Bath Terrace, and
now functions as
a daymark.

▼ An early 20th
century view from
the high light
showing the low
light, the South
dock, the West Pier
with lighthouse, and
lastly the East Pier
lighthouse.

The port of Blyth was formed around the river of the same name, and dates from the thirteenth century. By the eighteenth century, the west side of the river had developed into the area now known as Blyth, and a number of aids to navigation were erected to help guide vessels using the port.

In 1730, as well as a coaling quay, ballast quay, and pilots' watch house, a lighthouse had also been built at Blyth harbour. Little is known about this light, but in 1788 when the lighthouse known as Blyth High Light was built, it was reported that the harbour had been lit by two coal lights. The new lighthouse, built to the design of Sir Matthew White Ridley, was a 40ft tower lit by oil lamps and, when first built, was on the sea shore. However, due to land reclamation for the South Harbour, it is now about 100 yards inland at Bath Terrace.

As the South Harbour area developed, the light was obscured, so in 1858 the tower was increased in height to 54ft

and raised to its present height of 58ft in 1900. The light, which had a range of twelve miles, was converted to gas in 1857 and electricity in 1932. It shone from a window just below the top and, before it was discontinued in July 1984, served as the leading light for several harbour lights managed by Blyth Harbour Commission. Painted white, it now functions as a daymark.

The harbour was developed to the west by the construction of the North Pier in 1765 followed by the South Harbour in 1882. Two lights were built at this time, but the location of the second is unclear. The main protection for the harbour was the east breakwater on which a light was erected in 1884.

In 1906 the timber work and rubble of the breakwater were encased with concrete. By 1907 this breakwater had been extended by 900ft, and at the end the current leading light, known as Blyth East Pier Light or Harbour Light, was opened by John Whitfield, a harbour

Blyth

commissioner, on 18 July 1907. It consists of a 46ft white tapered monolithic concrete tower, with a gallery and lantern topped by a weather vane.

When first commissioned, the light had a third-order two-panel rotating prismatic lens driven by a clockwork mechanism and lit by a PV burner giving the upper lens a flashing white light every twenty seconds, with a range of twenty-one miles. A red light with a similar character had a range of seventeen miles. Beneath this was a third-order drum lens powered by a PV burner with a thirteen-mile range.

When later electrified, both lights were converted to LC lamp changers with 1,000-watt lamps. Monitoring was carried out by a hard wire connection to the harbour master's office. Recently, considerable energy saving and lamp life increases have been achieved by powering the light with seventy clear watt CDM-T lamps mounted inside both lenses, placed on PA2 lamp changers.

On 2 November 2008 a fire on the East Pier, after a firework display, damaged the cabling to the lighthouse, and an emergency generator was used for power until repairs were complete.

The other major works to the harbour consisted of the erection of the West Pier, which formed the eastern extremity of the South Harbour. In 1914 the work on a 'New' West Pier began. This was 350ft west of the original one, and was built to widen the harbour entrance and create a spreading basin for the waves so that swell did not range up the harbour. Due to the war, the work was not completed until 1922.

The new pier was built of timber on a rubble core, 1,450ft long, with the end section turning towards the East Pier to form a new harbour entrance. No date was recorded, but a lighthouse existed on the end of the original pier and this was re-erected on the terminal of the new pier. It consisted of a 15ft square metal tower with a fixed blue light shown through a window near

► An early 20th century view of the West Pier lighthouse which was later transferred to the new West Pier.

53852 Pier Head, Blyth. J.V.

the top. This light no longer exists, and has been replaced by a pair of small red lights mounted on a pole.

Prior to 1914, when the harbour entrance was altered, a low light was erected in the South Dock area to form a pair of leading lights, with the high light to mark the channel. This low light consisted of a 13ft hexagonal wooden tower with a small circular window near the top. In July 1984 both these lights were replaced by lattice towers, and the low light was presumably demolished.

Once vessels had entered the harbour a new course was required to manoeuvre upriver to the main harbour, and this was marked by a pair of range lights called Blyth Snook Front and Rear, situated on the east side of the river opposite Low Quay. Like the low light, they were 13ft hexagonal wooden towers with small circular windows

near the top. Presumably built before 1920, they exhibited fixed blue lights. The Front Range still exists, but the Rear Range is now a simple pole with a blue light and triangle on top.

At one time a lighthouse situated on the round end of the South Harbour was in operation. This consisted of a broad hexagonal metal housing on top of which was a small hexagonal lantern, which showed a fixed red light. The only clue to its age is a photograph taken in the early twentieth century.

▲ The lighthouse on the West Pier, was transferred to the new pier in 1922. The East Pier lighthouse can be seen in the background.

▼ The East Pier lighthouse erected in 1907 is now the main harbour light; the pier is also home to several wind turbines.

St Mary's

▶▶ The impressive
St Mary's lighthouse
is now a popular
tourist attraction.

▼ St Mary's
lighthouse north of
the Tyne is on an
island linked at low
tide by a causeway.

The lighthouse on St Mary's or Bait Island was established in 1898 to replace the lighthouse on the headland at Tynemouth Castle which had become obscured by pollution from the Tyne's industry and passing shipping. The tower, which was 120ft high, was constructed of brick by J. Livingston Miller and covered with cement render. The adjacent keepers' dwellings were constructed of stone and a covered passage connected them to the lighthouse. The pitched roofs were not added until the 1930s.

Operated by Trinity House, the light had a range of seventeen miles and was powered by paraffin vapour. Although electricity was provided to the island in 1957, it was not until 1977 that the lighthouse was converted to electrical operation. Automated in 1982, it was discontinued in 1984.

Today the island is a nature reserve and the lighthouse, now used as a visitor centre and souvenir shop, is open to the public. A climb of 139 steps to the top gives views across North Yorkshire and the North Sea. Access to the island is possible at low tide, but this was not always so. Before the first causeway was constructed in 1929, stepping-stones had to be used to cross the channel at low tide. Today's causeway dates from 1966.

In 2007 North Tyneside Council announced plans to spend £130,000 on improvement works to the lighthouse by renewing the electrical wiring, replacing broken lantern glazing and painting the exterior. The Council has also proposed to seek views on a master plan to preserve the island's existing structures and features, as well as provide additional amenities and facilities for visitors.

River Tyne

▶▶ The lighthouse
at the end of the
North Pier marking
the entrance to the
river Tyne.

▼ The North Pier
is open to the
public and shelters
a small beach at
Prior's Haven.

The river Tyne has been a centre for shipping and maritime trade for almost 2,000 years. During the industrial revolution, as the port expanded primarily to handle the region's growing coal trade, Newcastle became one of the country's major ports. The port no longer handles coal, but a variety of cargoes are brought up the Tyne, which remains a busy river marked by a number of lights.

Tynemouth Castle As early as the twelfth century, monks were reputed to have kept a light burning in the church tower on the headland on the north side of the river Tyne, in addition to a light in their priory on St Mary's Island, to help seafarers. In 1664, Colonel Villiers, Governor of Tynemouth Castle, replaced this light when he built a 79ft tower out of stone from the priory ruins

in the north-east corner of the grounds. The coal-fired light was shown from a roofed lantern room and the keeper's dwelling was in the base of the tower. It was probably established by patent some time after 1540. In 1581 a reference to it mentions 'the keeping of a continuous light in the night season . . . as in former times had been'.

In 1775 the lighthouse was partially rebuilt, before the light was changed to a revolving oil lamp with copper reflectors in 1802. Although the red light was often obscured by pollution from ships using the river, only after the Act of 1836, which empowered Trinity House of Newcastle to take over the lights in the area, could improvements be made. In 1898, after the lighthouse on St Mary's Island had been built, the Tynemouth Castle light was discontinued.

River Tyne

North Pier In easterly gales, it proved impossible for ships to enter or leave the Tyne so, in 1852, an Act of Parliament was passed which gave the Tyne Improvement Commission permission to build piers at the mouth of the river. Work started on the north pier in 1854 and should have been completed within seven years. However, a series of disasters resulted in the work lasting fifty years.

The pier was breached in 1867, when 1,900ft had been completed, and was breached again in 1897 after it had been completed to its final length of 2,959ft. It was found to be unstable and had to be rebuilt, and was eventually completed in 1910. The lighthouse on the end was constructed during the original build and was first lit on 15 January 1908.

Operated by the Port of Tyne, the light was shown from a 55ft circular stone tower complete with gallery and lantern, with the flashing white light visible for twenty-six miles. The lantern was made in Paris in 1890; the lens, one and a half tons in weight, floated in a bath of mercury. The tower also had a foghorn which gave a blast every ten seconds.

South Pier In comparison to the North Pier, the South Pier proved somewhat easier to build. However, gales during the 1860s hampered the work and, although construction had started in 1856, the pier and its lighthouse were not completed until 1895. The light is of similar design to that on the North Pier but, at 39ft, shorter.

The lantern and gallery railings are painted red, with the dome surmounted by a weather vane. The light, visible for thirteen miles, has three sectors – white, green and red – which show the safe channel into the harbour, with the green sector warning vessels of Bellhues Rock just over a mile to the north of the river.

▶▶ The South Pier lighthouse is the smaller of the two at the entrance to the river Tyne.

▼ The mouth of the Tyne, showing the South Pier (on left) and North Pier lighthouses.

North Shields

▶▶ The high light
situated above
North Shields Fish
Quay.

▼ The High and Low
Lights at Fish Quay.
In the middle is the
old light dating from
1727; located on
Beacon Street just
above Fish Quay, it
is now used as an
alms house.

The Tyne has always been a busy river, and the need to mark the river channel was apparent as early as the sixteenth century. In 1537, a request was made to Trinity House for a pair of lights to be erected at North Shields. These were initially candle-powered but, in 1727, Trinity House of Newcastle replaced them with a new pair of lights.

The low light was situated on the fish quay, with the high light at Beacon House, Trinity Buildings, 300 yards to the north-west. This light, which still exists, was a square four-storey building with a small lantern complete with a ball finial on an ogee-hipped roof. A two-storey extension was added later. Both these lights were powered by three candles until 1736, when they were increased in intensity by the installation of copper reflectors, and then in 1773 they were equipped with oil lamps.

In 1807, the lights had to be realigned, at which point the high light was discontinued. The low light was rebuilt on the same site to the design of John Stokoe, for Trinity House of Newcastle. It consisted of an 85ft six-storey square brick tower with a small lantern on the roof. The fixed white light, operated by the Port of Tyne, was visible for thirteen miles. In 1816 a two-storey red brick dwelling was added; today the site is a fish-curing plant.

In 1808 a new high light was erected in Dockray Square, also to the design of John Stokoe. The 58ft square four-storey white-painted brick tower had a wrought-iron balcony below a small lantern room on the roof. A two-storey dwelling was attached in 1860. The fixed white light was visible for sixteen miles. Both these towers are now daymarks as the lights have been discontinued. All three lighthouses are listed buildings and should be safe during any redevelopment of the area.

South Shields

ESTABLISHED
1882

CURRENT TOWER
1882

OPERATOR
Port of Tyne Authority

ACCESS
In fair weather it is
possible to walk the
groyne

▶▶ The distinctive
Herd Groyne
lighthouse at South
Shields with its
Hexagonal cone roof
and ball ventilator.

▼ Herd Groyne
lighthouse is one
of several aids to
navigation marking
the entrance to the
river Tyne.

Although the channel into the Tyne had been marked by a pair of lights on the north side since 1537, the south side was only marked by a pair of unlit beacons situated in South Shields. Known as East and West Lawe, they were built in 1832 by John Turnbull for £60 to replace earlier beacons. Still visible, they are tall obelisks, ashlar at the bottom with a brick upper section capped by a pyramid stone cap.

In 1854 the foundations of the North and South Piers were laid. Construction of the South Pier caused sand from Littlehaven beach to be swept up the river on the tide. To overcome this, a new groyne, called Herd Groyne, was erected in 1882 on the south side of the river. This extended from the river mouth at the northern end of Littlehaven beach, and not only deflected sand away from the river but also provided a south riverside marker for the

channel, which had been formed by the erection of the two piers.

To mark this channel, a lighthouse was erected on the end of Herd Groyne upon its completion in 1882. Situated almost opposite the North Shields lights, this light was displayed both upstream and downstream. It consisted of a 48ft red-painted corrugated iron service room on iron legs displaying the lights to seaward through a window in the lantern room, with the landward light shown from a separate lantern.

The seaward light, visible for thirteen miles, has an occulting white leading light which marks the river entry, together with red and green sectors. The landward light shows a fixed light for ships leaving the harbour. The light also carries a fog bell giving one stroke every five seconds. This light made the North Shields lights surplus to requirements.

Souter

ESTABLISHED
1871

CURRENT TOWER
1871

DISCONTINUED
1989

OPERATOR
Trinity House, now
National Trust

ACCESS
East of A183 main
road between South
Shields and Whitburn

▶▶ The impressive
tower at Souter
was one of many
designed by James
Douglass, Chief
Engineer to Trinity
House.

▼ The Souter
lighthouse at Lizard
Point, Marsden, seen
from the south.

Souter lighthouse was built to mark an underwater reef known as Whitburn Steel or Stile between the Tyne and the Wear. During the nineteenth century the seas off this part of the north-east coast became increasingly busy, with all kinds of vessels, ranging from coastal trading craft, carrying bulk cargoes such as coal and iron ore, to the expanding fishing fleets of the local ports. The dangers of the reef were highlighted on 16 November 1866, when the ship Sovereign from North Shields struck Marsden Rock. Although her eleven crew managed to scramble ashore to safety, the loss of Sovereign, together with a series of fatal shipwrecks that occurred during the next few years, highlighted the dangers of the reef.

To improve navigation in the area, Trinity House decided to build a new lighthouse at Lizard Point, Marsden. It was named Souter after the location originally chosen but then rejected, as a lighthouse named Lizard already existed (on Cornwall's south coast). The new station consisted of a 76ft red and white painted circular tower designed by James Douglass, Chief Engineer to the Corporation, and built by Robert Allison, of nearby Whitburn, from rubble masonry, which was covered in Portland cement to protect it from the weather.

The associated buildings, to landward of the tower, were laid out around a square courtyard with a covered inner courtyard and included an engine and boiler house, and workshop. The boilers needed large quantities of water, so rainwater tanks capable of holding 60,000 gallons were built into the foundations of the inner courtyard and by the engine room. Dwellings for the

Souter

lighthouse staff and their families were also built, and at one time more than thirty people were resident at Souter, including four keepers and an engineer, who was in overall charge.

Trinity House managed the station throughout its operational life. The lighthouse, which stood 345 yards from the cliff edge, entered service in January 1871, when Sir Frederick Arrow, Deputy-Master of Trinity House, stated that 'no lighthouse in any part of the world would bear comparison with it'. Visible for twenty-six miles, the white light flashed for five seconds at thirty-second intervals and was notable for being the first to be powered by electrical alternators.

These were the invention of Professor Holmes and proved very successful. The light they produced was magnified 230 times by a battery of lenses mounted in a rotating octagonal drum. This arrangement was used until 1914, when a new and larger lantern was installed and the light itself was converted from electricity to oil. In 1952 it reverted to electricity again, with power coming from the National Grid. The turntable was rotated by a weight-driven clockwork motor until an electrical system was installed in the 1970s.

The light was decommissioned by Trinity House in 1989 and the tower handed over to the National Trust. The Trust now maintains the lighthouse, which is open to the public, while it also still serves as a radio navigation beacon. The engine room, which originally housed Holmes' magneto-electric generators and two Cornish boilers supplied by Fairburn Engineering Co, remains just as it was when the station was handed over to the Trust.

Sunderland

▶▶ The elegant lighthouse at the end of Roker Pier.

▼ The 1856-built lighthouse was at the end of the South Pier until 1953 when it was moved here.

Before the New North, or Roker, Pier and New South Pier were constructed between 1885 and 1907, the entry into Sunderland port was guarded by what are now called the Old North and Old South Piers. A slender stone lighthouse was built in 1802 by J. Pickernell on the Old South Pier. It was replaced in 1856 and deactivated in about 1903, when the new pier lights made it redundant. In 1983 this pier was shortened and the lighthouse pictured below removed to Roker Cliff Park. Today, a 27ft red metal framework tower with a red flashing light visible for two miles, stands on the pier.

A light designed by Johnathan Pickernell was erected on the Old North Pier in 1802 and moved to the end by John Murray for the River Wear Commission when the pier was extended in 1841. Today, a 27ft yellow metal tower stands on the site showing a green light visible for eight miles. This light was upgraded and a fog signal installed in 2006. At the end of the New South Pier is a 33ft white metal tower with a white flashing light visible for ten miles.

The most noteworthy light is on the end of the New North Pier. Known as Roker Pier lighthouse, the conical granite stone-built 75ft tower is topped by a gallery and decorative white lantern with a black domed roof. It is built of alternating bands of naturally coloured stone to give a red and white appearance. Completed in 1903 by Henry Hay Wake for the River Wear Commissioners, it was reported to be the most powerful port light in the country. In 1976 the original prismatic lens was replaced by sealed beam units and moved to storage in the museum. In 2007 the mercury bed on which they rotated was removed and a modern low energy rotating lamp installed. The white light, now visible for twenty-three miles, flashes every five seconds.

The lighthouse on the Old South Pier built by Thorns Meik in 1856 was relocated in 1983 and now, known as Beacon Lighthouse, stands in Roker Cliff Park north of Roker Pier. The 50ft white circular wrought-iron tower with a cast-iron staircase is topped by a tall white lantern room with black gallery railings.

Seaham

▶▶ The 1905-built
lighthouse with
distinctive black and
white bands is a
notable landmark at
the end of the port's
north breakwater.

▼ The 58ft
lighthouse built in
1836 at Red Acre
Point as it was.

In the 1820s coal output from the Durham coalfield was increasing and additional export facilities were required. To meet this demand, the Marquess of Londonderry had the foundations for a new dock facility at Seaham laid in 1828, with the first coal exported from it in 1831.

To guide ships into the port, a wooden lighthouse was erected to the north of the dock entrance. In 1836 this lighthouse burnt down so later that year a new 58ft stone lighthouse was erected by William Chapman at nearby Red Acre Point. It had a revolving white light above with red light below. The first light keeper was William Fairless, who had fought against Napoleon.

In 1856 the interior of the tower burnt out, but it was restored a year later and the light continued to operate until 1905, when major harbour extensions made it redundant. The tower survived until 1940, when it was demolished as it was in the line of fire of the defence guns.

Part of the major alterations to the harbour in 1905 involved the construction of two long breakwaters. The northern one, which started close to the old lighthouse, extended 1,383ft to form, with the 876ft south breakwater, a new outer harbour. On the end of this breakwater a 33ft black cylindrical cast-iron lighthouse was built. It originally had a gallery below the lantern but this was removed during the 1960s. Today it shows a 1.2 second flashing green electric light visible for eleven miles, which is changed to fixed green in bad weather. The tower also carries a foghorn which sounds one blast every thirty seconds.

On the end of the South Pier is a 22ft high red pole which carries a fixed red light visible for five miles. There is a further red light visible for two miles on a 15ft red pole on the wave screen.

Hartlepool

HARBOUR

ESTABLISHED
1836

CURRENT TOWER
1899 (resited 1911)

OPERATOR
PD Teesport

ACCESS
The pier and
breakwater are open
to the public

▶▶ The entrance
to Hartlepool
harbour is marked
by a wooden square
lighthouse at the
end of the Old Pier.

▼ The first
lighthouse at
The Heugh,
on Hartlepool
Headland, was built
in 1847 and used
until 1915.

In 1201 the town of Hartlepool, built around a natural harbour, was granted a charter by King John, and it subsequently became the chief port for the powerful Bishops of Durham. In the Middle Ages it was the chief port for the area, but its prosperity declined and the harbour fell into disrepair until the nineteenth century. It was then developed as a port to handle the expanding coal export trade. A railway from Stockton, opened in 1841, went right into the docks, which were enlarged to accommodate the burgeoning trade.

What is now called the Old Dock was completed in 1835, with the new Victoria Dock opening in December 1840. The railway company then built a rival dock system, which resulted in West Hartlepool being created. The new Coal Dock opened in 1847 and expansion into Jackson Dock occurred in 1852. In 1967 the twin towns were united as the town of Hartlepool of today.

Hartlepool Harbour With an increase in trade and the additional shipping using the port, efficient aids to navigation were needed. By 1836 a new pier, now called Pilots Pier, had been built on the west side of the harbour entrance and a lighthouse was erected on its end. In 1899 it was replaced by the 38ft square pyramid-shaped wooden tower seen today.

This lighthouse was moved to its present position in 1911, when the pier was extended and a pair of leading lights erected on the pier head. Later a rotating radar antenna was erected on the top and the lighthouse and pier have recently been refurbished. The light flashes white every three seconds over the channel, and is otherwise green.

With the demise of the coal industry, the west docks fell into disuse and the Swainson Dock was filled in during 1968 and Central Dock in 1992. However, a major inward investment has

Hartlepool

SEATON CAREW

ESTABLISHED
1838

DISCONTINUED
circa 1884

ACCESS
The high light column is on display at Jackson's Landing by Hartlepool Marina

▶▶ The old Seaton high light tower, discontinued circa 1884, is now part of Hartlepool Marina minus its lantern. It was rededicated as a war memorial on 11 November 1997, and has eleven marble plaques around its base.

▼ A unique photograph of 1894 showing the now demolished Seaton Carew low light.

resulted in the transformation of the Old Coal Dock and Jacksons Dock area into a large marina and leisure complex, which opened in 1993. The entry to these docks has been improved by lock gates, with the approach via an outer refuge formed by two pairs of stone jetties. On the end of each there is a simple traffic control light on a pole, but the light on the outer North Pier is somewhat more substantial.

Seaton Carew To mark the Long Scar Rocks, which lay about a mile offshore, a pair of lights was erected at Seaton Carew in 1838. One was built half a mile inshore in Windermere Road, and the other was on the shore. The shore tower, Seaton low light, was a four-storey hexagonal tower with a balcony and lantern. It also had a hexagonal two-storey dwelling attached. It was painted white, with the corners and the conical roof black.

The Seaton high light consisted of a 70ft stone Tuscan column of Magnesian Limestone with stone balcony and lantern. Ships entering the Tees or Hartlepool would line up the red light from the high light with the white light from the low light for safe passage. When the lighthouse at South Gare was erected in 1884, however, these lights became obsolete and the low light was demolished. The high light fell into disrepair and the lantern was removed.

In the 1990s Hartlepool coal docks ware developed into a marina complex, which opened in 1993. In 1995 Teesside Development Corporation bought the old Seaton light and removed it, stone by stone, from within the grounds of a tin processing plant, and re-erected it at Jackson's Landing in Hartlepool Docks, minus its lantern.

The Heugh By 1846 Trinity House, spurred on by a

Hartlepool

▶▶ The lighthouse at The Heugh, a white-painted cast iron tower, dates from 1926-7. The headland is the site of the original town.

▼ The lighthouse at The Heugh, east of Hartlepool, is situated close to the gun battery and fort, gives two white flashes every ten seconds.

public meeting in 1844, was so concerned about the lights that they forced the Harbour Commissioners to replace the small light on the harbour pier with a lighthouse on the Heugh Headland. While the harbour light remained, three lighthouses were built on the Headland.

The first lighthouse was built in 1847 by Stephen Robinson and, sited on the cliff top at the Headland, was nearly 85ft above high tide. The 48ft tower was built of white sandstone and the lantern for the main light was powered by coal gas. The light was first exhibited on 1 October 1847 and had a range of eighteen miles. The lighthouse was probably the first to be lit reliably by gas, as the invention of a new type of burner made it possible to regulate the amount of air mixed with the gas to give a steady beam. The gas lamp with its Fresnel lens is now in the

Museum of Hartlepool.

In 1915 the first lighthouse was taken down because it stood in the way of the guns at Heugh Battery, and was replaced by a temporary wooden light on the Town Moor. This was a substantial 30ft high tapered square pyramid structure with the enclosed upper portion surmounted by the lantern and lens from the original lighthouse. It was in use until being replaced by the current light in 1927.

The current lighthouse, built in 1926-7, stands 42ft high and 62ft above high water, near the site of the first lighthouse. The white circular tower was built from welded steel plates. It was designed to be taken down in an emergency, something that almost happened during the Second World War when it was feared the Germans could use the lighthouse as a landmark, but the tower remained standing.

Teesmouth

The entry into the river Tees has always been challenging, and following a petition in 1883 two measures were taken to improve the situation. First, in 1884 the port authority built a 43ft circular cast-iron lighthouse on the eastern point of Salt Scar Rocks. Later, when the South Gare breakwater was constructed in 1888 to shelter shipping entering the Tees, lighthouse keepers' cottages were built part way along the breakwater and the light itself was incorporated into the knuckle on the northern end.

The light was made automatic in the 1960s and the keepers' cottages were then demolished.

Currently operated by PD Teesport, the tower is now painted white and shows a one and a half second long white flashing light every twelve seconds, which is visible for ten miles over the approach channel, with red sectors to each side. It is now a grade II listed building and, in 2007, became the first lighthouse in the UK to be fuelled by a hydrogen fuel cell.

Teesport is a busy port and improvements are continuous, with new investment in both facilities and aids to navigation. When the Norsea Terminal was built in 1975, a pair of navigation lights was erected to guide ships into the terminal. The front light consists of four high-intensity red lights in a square shown through a window at the top of a red and white banded circular concrete column. The rear light, 500m behind on a lattice tower, shows six red lights in a two wide by three high formation.

▶▶ The light at the end of the South Gare breakwater

▶ The South Gare lighthouse is in a compound closed to the public.

▼ The front range light within Teesport, on the north side at the Phillips Norsea Oil Terminal.

Whitby Harbour

▶▶ The light on the West Pier, the tallest of the harbour lights, was built in 1831 but has not been used since 1914.

▼ The picturesque entrance to Whitby harbour is marked by four lights of varying size and different dates.

Whitby, on the river Esk, was only a small village until, in the 17th century, the mining of alum shale in the surrounding area led to the need for larger vessels to transport the materials to process it. As a result, a shipbuilding industry flourished along the west bank of the inner harbour, bringing the need to improve the harbour entrance. This was achieved by replacing two wooden piers with two stone piers, the first of which, the West Pier, was commissioned by Sir Hugh Cholmley, Lord of the Manor, in 1632. The East Pier followed shortly after in 1702.

An exhibit in Whitby Museum of an ancient lantern shows a light which was exhibited on the West Pier until 1831. This lantern was hexagonal with four sides glazed, one side being a solid door and the sixth having a semi-circular groove so it could be strapped to a mast. It was lit by three candles, and the inside was polished to form a reflector.

From 1702 every passing collier paid a toll for maintenance of the piers, which were vital to Whitby's role as the only harbour of refuge on this coast. This income enabled the piers to be improved on a number of occasions, and in 1831 the original West Pier light was replaced by a fine new lighthouse consisting of an 83ft fluted yellow stone Grecian-Doric column with a square base. The white hexagonal lantern was mounted on a square stone gallery with white guard rails. Designed by Francis Pickernell, engineer to Whitby Harbour Trustees, it originally displayed a fixed green light visible for ten miles. After the pier extensions were built in 1914, it was shown only when a vessel was due and entry into the harbour was safe.

In 1855 a second lighthouse

Whitby Harbour

▲ The light on Whitby's West Pier extension shows a fixed green light.

▶▶ The East Breakwater lighthouse was built in 1855.

▶ The East Pier light on the pier extension at Whitby shows a fixed red light. There is no public access to this pier extension, although the light is easily viewed from the other side of the river.

was commissioned on the East Pier. It consisted of a 55ft fluted yellow stone Grecian-Doric column with a round base. The white hexagonal lantern was mounted on a round stone gallery with white guard rails and an ornate black roof. The light, visible for eight miles, showed a green fixed light with a red sector to indicate the wrong channel. It

was discontinued when the pier extensions were built and the red sector is now marked by a fixed red light on the church steps.

In 1914 the entrance was improved when pier extensions were constructed. Each was of stone with raised wooden sections, marked at their ends by light beacons. The West Pier light consists of a 26ft square wooden pyramidal support surmounted by a green lantern with a black top, which shows a fixed green light visible for three miles. The East Pier light, which displays a fixed red light visible for three miles, consists of a red lantern with black top, mounted on a 45ft square wooden pyramidal support. A foghorn on the end of the west extension sounds every thirty seconds during fog.

There is concern about the condition of the pier extensions and no public access is allowed on the East Pier extension.

Whitby

▶▶ Whitby
lighthouse is
situated to the
south of the town.

▼ The lighthouse
is on Ling Hill
overlooking the
North Sea. The fog
signal station can be
seen to the far left.

The lighthouse situated about two miles east of Whitby at Ling Hill is sometimes wrongly referred to by that name. When constructed in 1858 by Trinity House to James Walker's design, the station consisted of two towers which, when aligned, marked the dangerous Whitby Rock. The lower light, shown from a 66ft white octagonal tower with lantern and gallery, was deactivated in 1890.

The high light was refurbished and the 44ft white octagonal tower was equipped with a more effective light mounted in an octagonal lantern. The Whitby Rock was then marked by a red sector. Today the lamp is a first order catadioptric optic powered by three 250-watt tungsten halogen lamps mounted on a two-position lamp changer. The isophase light flashes every five seconds, with the white light visible for eighteen miles and the red sector for sixteen miles. The light was electrified in 1976 and the station automated in 1992.

The two single-storey keepers' dwellings attached to each side of the tower were redundant with automation and are now hired out as holiday lets. There was originally a fog signal giving four blasts every ninety seconds housed in an adjacent building with two large horns on the roof, but this has been discontinued.

In 1858 a Royal Commission on Lighthouses, with Admiral William Hamilton as chairman, visited lighthouses in Britain and France. It examined various proposals to improve the effectiveness of lighthouses, particularly their optical systems, and Whitby was chosen as the site for the tests. The new systems were made by the glass maker James Timmins Chance, working in conjunction with Michael Faraday.

Scarborough

ESTABLISHED
1806

CURRENT TOWER
1931

OPERATOR
Scarborough Borough
Council

ACCESS
The pier is open to the
public but the tower
is closed

▶▶ Scarborough
lighthouse on St
Vincent's pier.

▼ The lighthouse
in the old harbour,
overlooked by the
twelfth century
castle on the cliffs.

Scarborough has had a harbour since the eleventh century, and the West Pier was completed in 1325. However, it was not until after an Act of Parliament of 1732 that the present outer piers were built. The outer harbour was formed by the building of the Vincent Pier by William Vincent in 1752, with the East Pier some years later, in about 1811. Today the inner or old harbour is used by commercial traffic, with the outer harbour for leisure users.

In 1804 a signal flag was displayed on the end of Vincent's Pier, and in 1806 a circular brick lighthouse was built on the site. In 1843 it was raised in height by 17ft and a keeper's house attached to the seaward side. The light, visible for four miles, was displayed in a lantern room with a gallery. On 16 December 1914 the lighthouse was severely damaged by German Naval Forces and had to be demolished.

It was not until 23 September 1931 that its replacement, the current tower, was commissioned. Operated by the Borough Council since 1940, the 49ft white circular brick tower shows a main white isophase light in an octagonal domed lantern room, with a pair of vertically displaced fixed green lights to the seaward side. The light, visible for four miles, is supplemented by storm and tidal signals. The keepers' facilities are now used by Scarborough Yacht Club.

There are also lights on the end of both inner harbour piers. The quick flashing green East Pier light, visible for three miles, is on a 13ft tall mast, and the two vertical fixed red West Pier lights, visible for four miles, are on the roof of a 10ft high watch hut.

Flamborough

▶▶ The historic
octagonal
chalk tower at
Flamborough Head
had internal ladders.

▼ Flamborough
Headland with
the lighthouse on
the left and the
signal station to
the right.

An octagonal cylindrical white chalk tower, 79ft in height, was erected between 1669 and 1674 on high ground near the chalk headland of Flamborough Head to warn shipping of the dangers of the headland. King Charles II granted Sir John Clayton permission to build the tower for use as a beacon but, although it is said to be the oldest surviving light tower in England, it was in fact never lit. The building is well preserved, having served for more than three centuries as a daymark.

Clayton's chalk tower did not succeed in warning vessels of the dangers of Flamborough Head at night and, between 1770 and 1806, no fewer than 170 ships were wrecked off the headland. The Collector of Customs, Benjamin A. Milne, convinced Trinity House Brethren that such a disastrous loss of shipping could be prevented by a proper light built on the Headland.

As a result, a lighthouse to the design of Samuel Wyatt was constructed and first exhibited a light on 1 December 1806. The brick tower, 87ft in height with lantern and gallery, was built at a cost of £8,000 by John Matson, a builder of Prospect Street in Bridlington, who used no scaffolding and completed the work in nine months.

The tower was built with annular, stone internal steps, rising anti-clockwise and having unusually shallow risers. To accommodate the keepers, a two-storey house was built to the east of the tower. This is the only surviving lighthouse designed by Samuel Wyatt, who was consulting engineer to Trinity House from 1776 to 1807 and, between 1793 and 1795, designed their headquarters.

The original unique lighting apparatus was designed by George Robinson and consisted of a rotating vertical shaft to which were fixed twenty-one parabolic reflectors, seven on each of the three sides of the frame. Red glass covered

Flamborough

reflectors on two sides, giving for the first time a character of one white flash followed by two red flashes, which enabled vessels to distinguish it from Cromer, an innovation that was soon adopted elsewhere. The light was powered by oil, using Argand lamps with an equivalent candle power of 13,860.

In 1940 the lighthouse was electrified and further modifications took place in 1974. An electric fog signal was installed in 1975 to replace a diaphone apparatus. Originally a rocket was fired every five minutes during foggy weather. The lighthouse was automated in early 1996 and the keepers left on 8 May that year. The fog signal was refurbished and a standard fog detector now gives two blasts every ninety seconds. The light, 214ft above sea level, with its first order catadioptric rotating optic, shows four flashes every fifteen seconds and is visible for twenty-one miles.

The lighthouse has served as a waypoint for larger vessels and coastal traffic, and remains a prominent landmark. It also marks the Headland for vessels making for the small ports of Scarborough and Bridlington. The Headland itself, which is about six miles north-east of Bridlington, is a popular local tourist spot with a car park. The site is now managed by the East Riding of Yorkshire Council.

▶▶ The impressive lighthouse at Flamborough has a 'double gallery' which came about when the raised lantern on an iron gallery was fitted in 1924-25. The catwalk round the top of the murette to assist keepers cleaning the glazing is a unique feature of the design.

▶ Flamborough lighthouse is on a headland which is well signed from the village of Flamborough.

Bridlington

ESTABLISHED
1852

CURRENT TOWER
1852

OPERATOR
Bridlington Harbour
Authority

ACCESS
The pier is open to the
public

The harbour in Bridlington dates from medieval times. The wooden piers that formed the harbour were damaged and altered several times until, in the mid-nineteenth century, the stone piers were constructed which are in use today. The North Pier was completed in 1852 and on its end was placed a 28ft cast-iron column with a flashing white light, with a range of nine miles, in a lantern not unlike an old street lamp.

Although the column is not particularly noteworthy, it is somewhat ornate with a black trim to the white column and a red base which carries a life belt. The column also carries two further navigation lights operated by the Bridlington Harbour Authority. A similar cast-iron column is sited on the north harbour wall.

In 2008 proposals were agreed between East Riding of Yorkshire Council, Bridlington Harbour Commissioners and Yorkshire Forward to proceed with a scheme to provide a new harbour layout with a new marina, fishing harbour and improved facilities for pleasure boats. This will result in changes to the aids to navigation.

▶ The redundant light on the North Harbour wall, near the North Pier, is similar in design to the North Pier light.

▼ The ornate harbour light at Bridlington, with THV Patricia at anchor in the bay.

Withernsea

The architecturally unique 127ft octagonal brick tower with lantern and gallery is situated in Hull Road in the centre of Withernsea, an unusual setting for such a building. The lighthouse entered service in 1894 to help prevent the large number of shipwrecks that had occurred to many vessels which were travelling down the east coast, and which failed to see the lights at either Spurn or Flamborough. The additional light at Withernsea filled the gap.

When the lighthouse was built, only sand dunes and a mere separated it from the sea. Its unusual siting, evident today, came about after the promenade was extended along the sea front, and then houses were built on roads surrounding the tower. The lighthouse was therefore not originally built in the middle of the town, but some way back from the sea so that it would not become a victim of the erosion common on the east coast. With the building of the promenade, however, the threat of erosion was removed.

The lighthouse was established by Trinity House and was designed to work in conjunction with the Humber Lightship to guide vessels down the east coast and into the Humber Estuary. The construction work was undertaken by Strattens, of Edinburgh, between 1892 and 1894, taking eighteen months.

The tower itself has no dividing floors, and the inside is dominated by the spiral staircase, with its 144 steps, which leads to the service and lamp rooms at the top, as well as the light. Originally the light was oil-fired,

ESTABLISHED
1894

CURRENT TOWER
1894

DEACTIVATED
1972

OPERATOR
Withernsea
Lighthouse Trust

ACCESS
In the centre of the town, open to the public daily from March to October; access to the top of the tower is available

▼ The lighthouse at Withernsea dates from the late nineteenth century, when the town was developing.

The Light House. Hull Road.

Withernsea.

The Wrench Series, No. 5126

Withernsea

but in 1936 it was electrified, and had a range of seventeen miles. The lighthouse was discontinued on 1 July 1972.

In 1989 the lighthouse was taken over by the Withernsea Lighthouse Museum Trust and opened as a museum, mainly through the efforts of the Campbell family to house mementoes of Kay Kendall, a family member and film star of the 1950s. The base of the lighthouse contains a variety of displays of items of local interest, including the Humber and Withernsea lifeboats, as well as coastguards and shipwrecks, and the attached keeper's cottage is used as a café.

▶▶ The octagonal tower has at its base the spacious keepers' cottages. These are today used as a museum that is one of the best known tourist attractions in the Hull area, and the station itself is well maintained. It is possible for visitors to climb up to the lantern.

▶ The lighthouse at Withernsea as it was when in operation.

Spurn Point

▶▶ The stump of
the 1852 lighthouse
with water tank,
which was added
to the top after the
tower ceased to be
used as an aid to
navigation.

▶ The circular
compound with the
lightkeepers' houses
surrounding the
site of Smeaton's
high lighthouse. This
compound and the
houses have since
been demolished.

Spurn Point is a spit of sand and gravel about three miles long at the mouth of the Humber Estuary. It has both increased in length and moved westwards over time, and has been a danger to shipping using the river Humber and its various ports, the most important of which is Kingston-upon-Hull.

Lighthouses have been built on the Point since the early fifteenth century, making the area of considerable historical significance. The first information about a light on Spurn concerns a hermit, named William Reedbarrow, who in 1427 was given permission to charge dues for a light on a tower on Spurn Point. However, whether Reedbarrow finished his proposed tower, for which he was granted a letters patent in November 1427, or kindled his light, is not recorded.

In 1590 the Brethren of Hull Trinity House proposed a lighthouse on Spurn, but nothing came of this, and for most of the seventeenth century the Brethren opposed calls for lights to be built. Indeed, in 1632 they called lights 'Unusefull and needless'.

However, despite such attitudes, in 1674 a pair of coal-fired lights was erected on the Point, which was then two miles north of its current position. They were built by the London merchant Justinian Angell, who had a considerable legal battle with Trinity House at Hull before he succeeded in gaining permission to build the lights. These lights, known as high and low lights, were washed away several times, but the integrity of the high and low light strategy was necessary to mark the treacherous Humber Estuary.

The low light, originally a rudimentary pole with a basket of burning coal on top, was destroyed a number of times and resited to cater for the movement of the Humber's navigable channels. No reliable drawing of Angell's lighthouses exists, but, according to John Smeaton,

Spurn Point

▶▶ The 1895-built high lighthouse at Spurn Point remains a distinctive landmark, although it is disused and becoming derelict inside. The only lights on Spurn today are a flashing green starboard light on the end of the point, and fixed green lights marking the end of the pilot's jetty.

the high light was an octagonal tower built of brick, about 60ft high, with a coal fire in an iron basket hanging from a wooden lever or 'swape', with which the fire could be raised another 14ft.

By the middle of the eighteenth century the original lights, despite the lower one having to be moved or rebuilt several times, had become dangerously misleading, as Spurn Point had grown over a mile further south-west. An Act of Parliament was needed to override the objections of John Angell, grandson of the original builder, who still owned the rights to the light dues. Once this was passed, the engineer John Smeaton designed and had built two new lighthouses in 1776.

Smeaton's pair of coal-fired swape lights on brick towers, one 90ft and the other 50ft, were near the tip of the then point, with the high light visible for twelve miles. However, in 1892 cracks were discovered in the brickwork of the high light and three years later it was replaced

by the present 128ft brick tower, designed by the engineer to Trinity House, Thomas Matthews.

The low light built in 1776 gave good service until the 1810s, when the woodwork of the swape was found to have decayed so much that it needed to be replaced. Work on a new 50ft tower, equipped with an Argand lamp, started in July 1816. The tower, built by John Earle to the design of architect John Shaw, first exhibited a light on 25 November 1816. Another new low light had to be built in 1852 after the 1816 tower had been undermined by the sea.

However, the 1895 tower made the low light redundant, as three subsidiary fixed lights were shown from lower down the tower, so the lantern was removed altogether from the low light tower. Originally oil-fired, the high light had a range of seventeen miles, and flashed once every twenty seconds. It was converted to electricity in 1941, but was closed on 31 October 1985.

▶ The two lighthouses at Spurn Point as they are today, with the stump of Smeaton's 1776 tower on the beach and the 1895 tower among the sand dunes.

Thorngumbald Clough

ESTABLISHED
1870

CURRENT TOWER
1870

OPERATOR
Associated British
Ports Hull

ACCESS
Via a short walk along
the sea defence wall;
work is continually
being carried out on
the sea defences in
the area and access
may be affected

▶▶ Thorngumbald
Clough high light
with lantern and
service room.

▼ Thorngumbald
Clough low light on
the north bank of
the Humber.

Because of the Humber's ever-changing channels, by the 1860s the lighthouse at Paull no longer marked a safe passage through Paull Roads, and so in 1870 it was discontinued. In its place, a pair of lights was erected about half a mile east at Thorngumbald Clough.

The high light is a 50ft cast-iron framework red structure. The lantern, showing a white occulting light visible for eight miles, is housed in a red lantern room with a white domed top. The low light, 300ft away, is mounted on a 30ft white circular metal tower with a white domed lantern room on top. The white occulting light, displayed through a window, is visible for nine miles. The lights, when aligned, mark the safe channel for ships leaving the port of Hull. Vessels then realign with the lights at Killingholme on the south Humber bank to proceed to sea.

In 2003, following a breach in the sea wall between Paull and Thorngumbald, a decision was made to carry out a controlled land flooding scheme rather than repair the breach. This involved the area around the two lighthouses, and consideration was given as to whether to resite them. In the end, the sea defences on which they stand were reinforced by tons of large stones and the land behind them was sacrificed to the sea. They therefore now stand on a long stone promontory which is surrounded by sea.

The keepers' cottages, which were situated between the high and the low lights, were demolished in 1998.

Paull

ESTABLISHED
1836

CURRENT TOWER
1836

DISCONTINUED
1870

ACCESS
On the main road to
the sea front

►► Paull
lighthouse, now
stucco-covered,
was built by Trinity
House in 1836,
but was disused
by the end of the
nineteenth century.

▼ An old postcard
showing Paull
lighthouse and the
promenade along
the river Humber.

An aid to shipping, installed by Trinity House of Kingston-upon-Hull, has been at Paull since at least 1776, when a beacon was located north-west of the village. In 1831 Trinity House paid for the whitewashing of a house at Paull as a marker for ships, and four years later, as a temporary measure, they rented a room at the Humber Tavern in which they placed a lantern as a guide for vessels. Eventually they erected the white-painted 46ft conical brick tower situated on the street corner at Paull in 1836 at a cost of £60. The wardens for Trinity House at this time were William Collinson and George Hall.

The light was manned by a keeper paid £50 per annum, with an attendant paid £40. It was originally oil-powered, but was later changed to a gas burner, with the light displayed from a domed lantern room, the window of which faced the port of Hull. At this point the river channel is narrow due to sandbanks, and vessels leaving port had to navigate towards Paull lighthouse before changing course towards Killingholme lights on the south bank. Because the sandbanks shifted, the light was deactivated in 1870 and replaced by the two lights at Thorngumbald Clough.

The tower was originally freestanding in a space at the corner between the two terraces, but in 1820 a Mr Robert Thompson bought the land that the lighthouse is built on and subsequently extended the two terraces to join the tower.

After it was decommissioned, the lighthouse was handed over by Trinity House in 1909 to Humber Conservancy Board, who sold it at auction in 1947. A number of different people owned it, until in 1985 it was purchased by the present owner, who has extensively renovated it and turned it into a bed and breakfast establishment.

Salt End

ESTABLISHED
1870

AUTOMATED
1939

ACCESS
No trace exists today

In 1868 the Brethren of Trinity House of Hull, to better mark the deep water channel from No.13 Hebbles Buoy to Victoria Dock, erected two temporary lights on the river bank. These lights were successful, so they applied to Trinity House for permission for permanent lights.

As a result, two lighthouses at Salt End on the banks of the Humber were established in July 1870. This coincided with the deactivation of the lighthouse at Paul and the commissioning of the two lights at Thorngumbald. They were built by Thompson & Stather, of Hull, on land bought for £30 from the Humber Conservancy Commissioners.

The high light, a red-painted 54ft cylindrical tower, was of wrought-iron girders on masonry foundations, with a keeper's cottage adjoining. Access to the lantern was by spiral staircase leading to the storeroom, and then by iron ladder to the lantern.

The keeper appointed in 1877 was Fewson Hopper, who had been coxswain of the Spurn lifeboat and was father of James Hopper, landlord of the Lifeboat Inn at Spurn Point. The occulting white light, originally powered by oil lamps, was converted to electricity in 1926 and was visible for over twelve miles. It showed a fixed white light and an occulting white light of four seconds on and two seconds off.

The moveable low light was a white wrought-iron 22ft cylindrical tower. It was originally powered by oil lamps but was converted to electricity in 1926. The light was fixed white, with a range of ten miles. By 1939 the lights were unattended and no keeper was employed. The lights fell into disuse with the building of new jetties for the British Petroleum Oil Terminal in the 1960s, and were demolished. Today simple lights on poles are on each of the three oil jetties.

► The old lights at Salt End are no longer in existence. The low light was originally mounted on a trolley which ran on rails 21ft long so that it could be moved along a north-south axis in front of the high light to ensure the shifting sand banks were accurately marked. The light was moved slightly on its rails in 1893 and in 1897 a red sector light was added to cover the Skitter Sand Elbow.

Spurn Light Vessel

As well as the land-based aids to navigation on the Humber, manned light vessels were also located along the river, from beyond Spurn Point to west of Hessle at Hebbles, as early as 1820. One position was off Spurn Point, where LV-16 initially served as Spurn Light Vessel.

Built in 1927 for the Humber Conservancy Board by the Goole Shipbuilding and Repairing Co at a cost of £17,000, it was towed into position in the estuary on 17 November 1927 to act as the first aid to navigation at this location. The vessel is partitioned into three areas: the crew's living quarters with four sleeping berths, a wash area, and a kitchen unit. The rotating light was oil-powered, with parabolic reflectors as well as a foghorn.

In 1959 a new light vessel was under construction for Spurn so LV-16 was reallocated to become Bull Light Vessel. Before going there, she was surveyed and repainted red, having been black while at Spurn. She was decommissioned from Bull in November 1975 and sold to Hull City Council in 1983. In February 1987 she went to Hull Marina.

On the 28 June 1959 the new light vessel LV-14 was towed out to Spurn to replace LV-16. She was built at Cook, Welton and Gemmell's Yard in Beverley and had accommodation for seven crew. The rotating light, which was initially oil fuelled, had a prism lens as opposed to the usual parabolic reflectors. The light was later converted to electric operation. After being decommissioned on 11 December 1985, she was sold to Guernsey, then went to Conwy in 1988, then to Milford Haven and later Waterford, before being towed by her present owners to Sharpness.

ESTABLISHED
1927

LAST VESSEL
1959

DEACTIVATED
1985

OPERATOR
Hull City Council

ACCESS
Original light vessel on display at Hull Marina, Castle Street, Hull; open April to September

▼ Built from steel, LV-16 was restored to her original condition in the 1980s and taken to Hull Marina, where she is open to the public from March to September.

River Ouse

Although a number of beacons and small lights guide vessels using the river Ouse, only two can be described as lighthouses. One, at Whitgift, also known as Whitgift Bight, consists of a slightly tapering white-painted 46ft brick tower on an unpainted hexagonal brick base on the flood bank of the river. Its red light, visible for five miles, gives two flashes every four seconds from a small polycarbonate lantern on the balustrade of the dome-roofed lantern.

The other light, Apex, is situated in the river channel three miles east of Whitgift at Trent Falls, where the rivers Ouse and Trent converge to become the Humber. Mounted on the end of the training wall, it was erected in 1933 by the Lower Ouse Improvement Trustees and consisted of a red 40ft elaborate circular steel tower on a sturdy square wooden base. Sometimes known as Trent Falls lighthouse, it was powered electrically from the Trust's power plant on the north side of the river at Blacktoft, with an acetylene light as back-up.

The light was a fourth order dioptric group triple flashing, showing three periods of half a second on, one second off, half a second on, one second off, half a second on, with a final six and half seven seconds off, every ten seconds. It had a white sector for entry into the Trent visible for ten miles, and a red sector visible for six miles for entry to the Ouse. In addition, the lighthouse had a diaphone foghorn operated by compressed air. This gave a blast of one and three quarter seconds every twelve seconds, with an electric siren for use as a back up.

This lighthouse is now preserved and on display at the Waterways Museum in Goole. Its replacement consists of a steel tube which supports a simple green flashing light on the end of the training wall.

▶▶ Whitgift lighthouse on the south bank of the river Ouse stands six miles east of the port of Goole. The tower was refurbished in 2008.

▶ The refurbished apex light on display next to the No.5 Coal Hoist at Goole Docks as part of the nearby Waterways Museum.

Killingholme

ESTABLISHED
1836

CURRENT TOWER
1836, 1851, 1876

OPERATOR
Grimsby &
Immingham Port
Partnership

ACCESS
Via the sea wall,
which protects all
three lighthouses

▶▶ The South
low lighthouse at
Killingholme helps
to guide vessels in
the river Humber.

▼ The Killingholme
lighthouses with the
High and South low
lights foreground
left and the North
low light in the
background.

To the north of Killingholme are three lighthouses, the High, North and South low lights, to mark a safe passage along the busy river Humber. The high light, a red-painted stucco-covered tapering conical 79ft tower, was one of two lights commissioned by the Kingston-upon-Hull Trinity House in 1836. The occulting red light, flashing every four seconds and visible for fourteen miles, is shown through a window housed in a domed lantern room, around which is a gallery.

Originally operating in conjunction with both the North and South low lights, it now marks the entry into the lower reaches of the Humber Estuary, in conjunction with the south low light, and helps to guide vessels clear of the sandbanks between Killingholme and Spurn. Prior to the decommissioning of Spurn Point lighthouse, it operated in conjunction with that also.

On 4 June 1875 the high lighthouse was struck by lightning, which caused considerable damage, and part of the dome over the lantern was ripped way. Temporary repairs were carried out and a survey found that the stonework was decaying and the foundations were weak. As a result, in March 1876, the Brethren of Trinity House invited tenders for taking down the lighthouse and its cottage and having them re-erected on the same site. The new lighthouse had a larger base and thicker walls than the old building, and its construction was completed at a cost of £2,675. Two temporary lights were shown during the building of the new tower, and these were dismantled in December 1876 when the light from the new tower was shown for the first time.

The South low light, which was also erected in 1836, is a white-painted stucco-covered 46ft tapered conical brick tower. It shows a flashing Isophase red light, one second on, one second

Killingholme

▶▶ The red-painted Killingholme high light now stands in the grounds of a sewage works.

▼ Killingholme North low light, now unused, has a single-storey keeper's house attached, which is used as a private residence.

off, visible for eleven miles, and displayed through a window in a white-domed lantern room. Like the high light, it has a gallery around the lantern room and, although neither tower has an adjoining building, each has a set of chimneys running up the tower and protruding above the dome. Although little is known about him, Francis Dales is recorded as the designer of this and the light at Paull, both of which were built in the same year.

The North low light, 800 yards to the north, was built in 1851 and consisted of a 46ft white-painted stucco-covered tower and attached dwelling house. The light, visible for eleven miles, was displayed through a window in a white lantern room with black

domed top. Like the other two lights, it also has a gallery and set of chimneys. Decommissioned in 1920, the lighthouse was used as a signal station prior to the establishment of the coastguard station, and has now become a private dwelling. The lighthouses once dominated the landscape, but they are now dwarfed by nearby oil refineries, power station and sewage works.

In 2005 Associated British Ports was looking to replace the present 292-degree leading lights at Killingholme, which can be obscured by vessels at the Immingham oil berths. In 2006 a sector light was added to the high light to try to alleviate the problem, and since then no further changes have been made.

Glossary

▲ The original 1895 rotating lens used in Spurn lighthouse. It had a range of seventeen miles, and was replaced in 1956-57.

Acetylene A highly combustible gas which burns with an intensely bright flame.

Argand lamp A bright and relatively clean-burning lamp invented by Francois-Pierre Ami Argand in 1783.

Automated An unmanned light controlled externally; all the major UK lighthouses are automated with Trinity House controlling and monitoring its lights from the Corporation's depot in Harwich.

Beacon A structure, usually land based, either lit or unlit, used to guide mariners.

Catadioptric lens A dioptric lens with additional outer prisms,` which reflect then refract light beams to give added intensity

Character The identifying feature of a lighthouse is its character; for example the light could be described as fixed, or flashing.

Daymark Light towers often also serve as daymarks, which are fixed unlit beacons visible from the sea and marking a navigational hazard.

Dioptric lens A development by Augustin Fresnel consisting of a bull's eye lens surrounded by a series of concentric glass prisms which concentrate the beam by refraction. Dioptric lenses are classified by their focal length.

Elevation The elevation refers to a light's height above sea level; the higher the elevation, the greater the range.

Flashing light A light where the period of light is less than the period of darkness.

Fog signals A sound signal used to warn mariners in times of fog or heavy weather.

Gallery The external walkway encircling the lantern or the lantern room.

High light The taller or higher of a pair of lights.

Isophase light A light where the periods of light and dark are equal.

Keepers The persons responsible for maintaining and keeping the light at an aid to navigation, including the associated buildings.

Lanterns The glass-enclosed space at the top of a lighthouse housing the lens or optic; lanterns are often encircled by a narrow walkway called the gallery.

Light vessel A vessel built to support an aid to navigation.

Low light The shorter or lower of the two lights used to mark a channel or hazard.

Occulting Where the period a light exhibited is greater than its period of eclipse; this can be achieved in several different ways.

Range lights Lights in pairs which mark a channel.

Reflector A system which intensifies light by reflecting the light source into a beam, both to increase intensity and to enable the beam to be manipulated to produce differing light characters.

Training wall A bank or wall erected below water level in a river or harbour mouth to train the water flow.

Bibliography

Boer, G. de: A History of the Spurn Lighthouses (East Yorkshire Local History Society, 1968).

Bowen, J. P.: British Lighthouses (Longmans, London, 1947).

Hague, Douglas B. and Christie, Rosemary: Lighthouses: Their Architecture, History and Archaeology (Gomer Press, Dyfed, 1975).

Jackson, Derrick: Lighthouses of England and Wales (David & Charles, Newton Abbot, 1975).

National Trust: Souter Lighthouse and The Leas (The National Trust, 1995).

Nicholson, Christopher: Rock Lighthouses of Britain (Patrick Stephens, Somerset, 1995).

Storey, Arthur: Trinity House of Kingston-upon-Hull (Trinity House, Hull, 1967).

Williams, Peter: Beacon on the Rock (Quintet Publishing Limited, London, 2001).

Woodman, Richard and Wilson, Jane: The Lighthouses of Trinity House (Thomas Reed Publications, 2002).

Websites

www.lighthousedepot.com
Comprehensive list of world lights with details, photos, locations and links.

www.trabas.de/enindex.html
List of world lights including minor lights with photos.

www.unc.edu/~rowlett/ lighthouse/index.htm
Comprehensive list of world lights with historic outline, photographs and links.

www.trinityhouse.co.uk
Trinity House website with details of all their lighthouses.

www.michaelmillichamp. ukgateway.net Main focus is on England and Wales with details of operational and non-operational lights.

Acknowledgements

Many people have assisted with the compilation of this book and our thanks for to Vikki Gilson, at Trinity House, for her continued help and support; Gerry Douglas-Sherwood of the ALK, for his knowledge; Coxswain Dave Steenvoorden, at Spurn Point; Paul Hood, at Blyth; Bob Williams, at Hartlepool; Peter Bendall and Natasha Singleton.

All photographs and images are by Nicholas Leach, except the following: Tony Denton pages 60 (upper), 74 (upper); supplied by Michel Forand 6 (upper), 9, 11 (both), 12 (lower), 34, 52, 75, 84 and 86; Association of Lighthouse Keepers 20 and 22; Paul Hood 8, and supplied 32 and 35 (upper); Trinity House 6 (lower), 12 (upper), 30, 72 and 94; supplied by Jeff Morris 78; Sallyann Anderson 2; and Cliff Crone 37.

Finally, thanks as ever to Maureen and Sarah for their patience and support during our continued researches and visits to the country's lighthouses.

Index